Television

Identifying Propaganda Techniques

Curriculum Consultant: JoAnne Buggey, Ph.D.
College of Education, University of Minnesota

By Carol O'Sullivan

OPPOSING
JUNIORS
VIEWPOINTS®

Greenhaven Press, Inc.
Post Office Box 289009
San Diego, CA 92128-9009

Titles in the opposing viewpoints juniors series:

AIDS	The Palestinian Conflict
Alcohol	Patriotism
Animal Rights	Poverty
Death Penalty	Prisons
Drugs and Sports	Smoking
The Environment	Television
Gun Control	Toxic Wastes
The Homeless	The U.S. Constitution
Immigration	Working Mothers
Nuclear Power	Zoos

Cover photo: © Sandy Roessler/FPG International

Library of Congress Cataloging-in-Publication Data

O'Sullivan, Carol, 1945
  Television : identifying propaganda techniques / by Carol
O'Sullivan.
    p. cm.—(Opposing viewpoints juniors)
  Summary: Explores the use of critical thinking to analyze
differing views about the effects of television on children in the
home and in the classroom.
  ISBN 0-89908-606-3
  1. Television and children—Juvenile literature. 2. Propaganda—
-Juvenile literature. [1. Television. 2. Propaganda.] I. Title.
II. Series
HQ784.T4084 1990
302.23'45'083—dc20   90-3785
                                      CIP
                                        AC

CONTENTS

THE PURPOSE OF THIS BOOK

An Introduction to Opposing Viewpoints

When people disagree, it is hard to figure out who is right. You may decide one person is right just because the person is your friend or a relative. But this is not a very good reason to agree or disagree with someone. It is better if you try to understand why these people disagree. On what main points do they differ? Read or listen to each person's argument carefully. Separate the facts and opinions that each person presents. Finally, decide which argument best matches what you think. This process, examining an argument without emotion, is part of what critical thinking is all about.

This is not easy. Many things make it hard to understand and form opinions. People's values, ages, and experiences all influence the way they think. This is why learning to read and think critically is an invaluable skill.

Opposing Viewpoints Juniors books will help you learn and practice skills to improve your ability to read critically. By reading opposing views on an issue, you will become familiar with methods people use to attempt to convince you that their point of view is right. And you will learn to separate the authors' opinions from the facts they present.

Each Opposing Viewpoints Juniors book focuses on one critical thinking skill that will help you judge the views presented. Some of these skills are telling fact from opinion, recognizing propaganda techniques, and locating and analyzing the main idea. These skills will allow you to examine opposing viewpoints more easily. The viewpoints are placed in a running debate and are always placed with the pro view first.

What Are Propaganda Techniques?

Propaganda is information presented in an attempt to influence people. In this Opposing Viewpoints Juniors book, you will be asked to identify and study two common propaganda techniques. These techniques might appeal to your ability to think logically, or they might appeal to your emotions. As an example, a car salesperson who is telling you about a small economy car may say, "This car gets much better gas mileage than any other car in its class." The salesperson's argument is based on his belief that you will make your car-buying decision logically. You will compare practical considerations such as mileage and initial cost. Another example is a car salesperson who is telling you about a snazzy Maserati: "This car is the best-looking, fastest car ever made." Her argument for buying the Maserati is based on her belief that you are considering such a car not for its practical qualities but because it excites you and is a status symbol.

In the examples above, the objective of both salespeople is to encourage you to buy a car. Both try to get you to focus on the most appealing qualities of their cars—economy in the first example, flashiness in the second. Both ignore the disadvantages of their cars. In both cases, making a wise buying decision would mean getting more information. Since the car salespeople's objective is to get you to buy one of *their* cars, you would need more objective sources, such as *Consumer Reports* magazine, to find out more facts.

DISTRACTING THE READER

All propaganda techniques, like those used by the car salespeople, distract the listener or reader from the complete picture. People who use propaganda techniques encourage you to look only at the factors that are important to accepting their argument as true.

Authors and speakers often use misleading propaganda techniques instead of offering legitimate proof for their arguments. The propaganda will be offered as a reason to believe the argument, but in reality it will be weak, distracting, or irrelevant reasoning. This Opposing Viewpoints Juniors book will focus on helping you tell the difference between legitimate reasons to believe a particular argument and propaganda techniques that are used to mislead or distract you.

It is important to learn to recognize these techniques, especially when you are reading and evaluating differing opinions. This is because people who feel strongly about an issue use many of these techniques when attempting to persuade others to agree with their opinion. Some of these persuasive techniques may be relevant to your decision to agree or not, but others will not be. It is important to sift through the information, separating the proof from the false reasoning.

While there are many types of propaganda techniques, this book will focus on two—*generalization* and *strawperson.*

Generalization—a statement that suggests that all members of a group are the same in some way. A generalization denies that some members of the group may be different. For example, "Everyone likes to play outside" denies the possibility that some people do not like to play outside. Or the statement "Truck drivers listen to country music" implies that all truck drivers listen to country music when, in fact, some truck drivers may never listen to country music.

Generalizations can also apply to places and things. For example, "The world's beaches are polluted with plastic debris" is a generalization. It implies that all beaches everywhere are littered with plastic. But many are not.

Generalizations often use facts or statistics to back up a statement that applies to all members of a group. For example, "Sixty percent of the people I talked to at the convention favored a debate between the candidates." The conclusion the speaker wants you to arrive at is that most people at the convention favored a debate. But the speaker may have talked to only ten people, and there may have been thousands of people attending the convention. In that case, ten people is not a large enough sample to indicate that most people favored a debate.

People who use generalizations often cite an example in which the situation is true in one instance to convince you that it is true all the time. For example, a person may say, "Teenagers are careless drivers. This morning I saw a teenager weaving in and out of traffic and driving about twenty miles over the speed limit. He finally flipped his car, injuring himself and his passengers." The speaker hopes to convince you that because one teenager drove carelessly, all teenagers do.

Strawperson—presenting a distorted or exaggerated form of the opponent's argument in order to make it sound illogical or silly. An example is "Senator Jones favors a study of the effects of acid rain before any definite steps are taken to correct it. He apparently wants to wait until acid rain has destroyed all the world's lakes and forests before doing anything about it." The speaker presents Senator Jones's real argument about studying acid rain—that Senator Jones favors further study of acid rain before steps are taken to correct it. Then the speaker distorts the argument to make it sound ridiculous. He says that Senator Jones wants to wait until acid rain has destroyed all the lakes and forests in the world before doing anything about it. This is not what Senator Jones said.

Not all cases in which a person criticizes an opponent's argument are examples of setting up a strawperson. Some are legitimate rebuttals to the argument. For example, an opponent of Senator Jones's argument to wait for further study on acid rain might make a good argument against waiting. He might say, "Senator Jones favors waiting before dealing with acid rain. But last year, four thousand more lakes died from acid poisoning. And ten thousand new forests were added to the list of woodland areas being destroyed by acid rain. If acid rain destruction continues at this rate, in five years over 50 percent of the world's lakes and forests will have died from acid rain." This is not a strawperson argument. It is a rational rebuttal to Senator Jones's argument.

SOUND REASONING VS. PROPAGANDA

When reading differing arguments, then, there is a lot to think about. Do the authors give sound reasons for their points of view? Or do they misrepresent the importance of their arguments with generalizations? Do the authors point out existing flaws in their opponents' arguments? Or do they set up a straw version of their opponents' arguments to make them seem ridiculous?

We asked two students to give their opinions on the effects of television on children. Look for examples of generalization and strawperson in their arguments:

I think kids should be allowed to watch as much TV as they want.

Television shows are based on real life. All kids who watch television learn what the world is really like. Sure, lots of creepy things happen on TV. People get murdered. They steal from each other. They take drugs. But people do this in real life, too. Kids need to learn about these things so they'll know what to do if something bad happens to them. For instance, if someone tries to get a kid to take drugs, the kid will know not to do it. He or she will have learned how dangerous drugs are by watching television.

My mom says kids shouldn't be allowed to watch violent television shows. She says some kids act like the people they see on television. When kids see some guy hitting another guy, they think it's okay to hit their little sister or brother.

I think mom is wrong. I don't think all kids who watch violent television programs grow up thinking they can beat up everybody to get their own way. Most of them grow up to be pretty normal.

I think parents should forbid kids to watch some TV shows.

My big brother watches "Roseanne" every week. On that show, the kids talk back to their parents all the time. After he watches "Roseanne," my brother talks back to my parents. My parents get angry with him and punish him. Then everybody in the house gets upset, including me and my little sister. I think my brother should be forbidden to watch "Roseanne"; then he wouldn't learn to talk back to my parents.

I don't think television producers should make shows where the kids talk back to their parents. But some producers say they have to make shows people like or people won't watch television. And according to these producers, people like to watch families yelling at each other.

This argument doesn't make sense to me. People like all sorts of things that are bad for them and that they shouldn't be allowed to have. Kids like candy. Should their parents let them have candy for breakfast, lunch, and dinner just because they like it? No. And kids should not be allowed to watch all the TV shows they want either.

ANALYZING THE
SAMPLE VIEWPOINTS

Christopher and Kelly have very different opinions about whether children should be allowed to watch certain television programs. Both of them use propaganda techniques in their arguments.

Christopher:

GENERALIZATION

All kids who watch television learn what the world is really like.

STRAWPERSON

Mom's argument: Some kids who watch violent television shows act like the people they see on television.

Christopher's distortion of the argument: I don't think all kids who watch violent television programs grow up thinking they can beat up everybody to get their own way.

Kelly:

GENERALIZATION

On "Roseanne," the kids talk back to their parents all the time.

STRAWPERSON

The producers' argument: We have to make shows people like or they won't watch television.

Kelly's distortion of the argument: People like all sorts of things that are bad for them and that they shouldn't be allowed to have. Kids like candy. Should their parents let them have candy for breakfast, lunch, and dinner just because they like it?

After reading these sample viewpoints, what would you conclude about parents limiting the television shows their children can watch? Why? As you continue to read through the viewpoints in this book, keep a tally like the one above to compare the authors' arguments.

CHAPTER 1

PREFACE: Does Television Harm Children?

Watching television has become a favorite form of entertainment in the United States. Many children spend up to one-third of their waking hours in front of a televison screen. What effect watching so much television has on children is a subject often debated by psychologists, educators, and the general public.

One theory holds that television is a wonderful invention that can serve as educator, entertainer, baby-sitter, and companion to children. According to Fred Rogers, of "Mr. Rogers' Neighborhood," television is beneficial to children. He says that television is a "marvelously wonderful thing" that can be used to nurture, to stimulate imagination, and to educate. He adds that television demonstrates "how problems can be worked on and often solved by mutual respect."

Other people are not so optimistic about the benefits of television. Marie Winn, author of "The Plug-in Drug," believes that television is harmful to children. On the physical level, she says, watching television prevents children from getting enough exercise. Their bodies become weak and underdeveloped. On the mental level, television deadens children's imagination and their ability to think. Television programs simply feed the story to the children without giving them an opportunity to imagine what might happen next.

A third opinion, offered by the U.S. Department of Education, is that television has little effect on children. This is because they engage in other activities while they watch television. They eat, talk, do homework, play games, and daydream. In short, television has little effect on children because children do not pay attention to the programs they are watching.

The effects of television on children is a heated issue. Arguments for and against it use many propaganda techniques. In the next two viewpoints, look for examples of generalization and strawperson.

Editor's Note: In this viewpoint, the author defends television. She argues that television teaches children facts about the world as well as values that will help them live in the world. As you read, watch for propaganda techniques the author uses to convince you that she is right.

The author's claim that television critics blame television for all society's ills is an example of strawperson. The real argument is that television teaches children disrespectful and violent behavior.

A common complaint among some people in our society today is that television is bad for children. They claim it teaches children disrespectful and violent behavior to get their way. These people seem to think that television is to blame for all society's ills.

I disagree that television is bad for children. I think television teaches children many useful things. Most television shows teach them something about the world they live in, such as the foods African animals eat. Other shows teach them about the jobs people do for a living or about how airplanes fly.

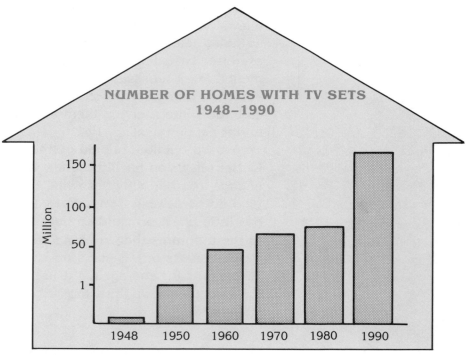

NUMBER OF HOMES WITH TV SETS
1948–1990

SOURCES: Engage/Social Action 1987 & The Nielsen Report on Television 1988

Famous people agree that television is good for children. Isaac Asimov, the writer, tells about the time he first realized what an effective teacher television can be. When he received a large silver bowl as a gift, his young son recognized it as a champagne cooler. Asimov asked his son where he had learned about champagne coolers. He replied that he saw them all the time on "The Three Stooges."

Besides teaching children facts about their world, television also teaches children to treat other people with kindness. In an episode of "Family Ties," Alex, the teenage son, and his younger sister, Mallory, both enter the same contest. They each have to make something that represents the type of career they want to enter.

As usual, Alex wins—the prize is a scholarship to college. Alex knows that Mallory came in second. In order to build her self-esteem, he drops out of the contest, and Mallory wins the scholarship. For Alex, Mallory's happiness more than makes up for the loss of the scholarship. This show and others like it teach children to consider other people's feelings first. They teach children that their own happiness comes from making other people happy.

One complaint television critics have about television is that it presents a fantasy world to children. They say that the problems on TV are too easily and too quickly solved. Serious problems, such as drug abuse and teen pregnancy, are worked out in an hour. In real life, these problems take months, even years, to work out.

But teaching children that problems can be easily and quickly solved is good for them. It helps them believe in happy outcomes. It gives them the sense that life's problems can be overcome. Child Psychologist Bruno Bettelheim agrees. He says the quick solutions to problems on television help "shape children's expectations for the world, and also their coping skills when faced with difficulties."

People who say television is bad for children obviously do not watch television. If they did, they would realize that it is educational. I cannot understand why these people want to rob children of things that educate them and bring them pleasure.

Isaac Asimov's personal experience does not prove that all famous people agree that television is good for children. The author is making a generalization about an entire group of people based on the experiences of one person.

To support her argument that television teaches children to treat other people with kindness, the author cites an example from one episode of one television program. Is this a generalization? Why or why not?

The author is implying that teaching children quick solutions to problems is good for all children. She discounts the fact that some children may not benefit from such instruction. Which propaganda technique is she using?

The author is implying that television critics never watch television. Which propaganda technique is she using?

Television as teacher

Do you agree with the author that television provides children with useful knowledge? Why or why not? Name some facts you have learned from television. Do you consider these facts useful? Why or why not?

Editor's Note: This viewpoint argues that television harms children because it teaches them useless information and socially irresponsible moral values. The author cites concrete examples to support his argument. As you read, be aware of the author's attempts to persuade you. Take note of which propaganda techniques he uses.

Are all television programs filled with violence and sex? Is this a generalization? Why or why not?

The author is implying that all children's programs teach children bad habits. He cites "Sesame Street" as an example. Is this a propaganda technique? If so, which one?

Is this a distorted version of the argument set forth by the defenders of "Sesame Street"? What is their real argument? Which propaganda technique is this?

I believe watching television is bad for children. Television programs are filled with violence and sex. Children learn from these programs. They learn to use violence to get their way. They learn that sex without marriage is an acceptable form of recreation.

Even programs made especially for children, although they do not include sex and violence, teach children bad habits. For example, Cookie Monster on "Sesame Street" teaches children to be impolite. He grabs cookies away from other people and stuffs them into his mouth. He talks with his mouth full, and he does not even use proper grammar. "Me want cookie," he shouts, spitting cookies all over the place.

The people who defend this program claim that Cookie Monster's behavior is exaggerated on purpose. By watching Cookie Monster behave like a slob, children see how disgusting he is. This keeps them from behaving like Cookie Monster. I do not understand the logic of this argument. That is like saying that watching people rob banks on television will prevent children from becoming bank robbers.

Reprinted with special permission of North American Syndicate, Inc.

Another thing television teaches children is that money and beauty are the most important qualities a person can have. In the program "Facts of Life," Blair is the wealthy roommate of Joe, Tootie, and Natalie. Even though Blair is snobbish and self-centered, she has boys falling all over themselves to be with her. Tootie, Joe, and Natalie are much nicer than Blair, but they seldom have dates.

The author is making a generalization about what television teaches children. What is this generalization? What evidence does he use to support it?

Some people claim that television teaches children other things besides rudeness and poor values. They claim that children learn new words and new ideas from television. Perhaps they are right. But what children learn is useless information. They learn to sing idiotic commercial jingles and to say silly words like "yabba dabba doo," and "sufferin' succotash."

Is this a generalization? Why or why not?

These bits of information will probably not help children get along in the world. I cannot think of a single instance in which being able to sing "Oh, I wish I were an Oscar Mayer wiener" would be of help to anyone. But people who are pro-television insist that the more useless information kids learn, the better equipped they will be to deal with life.

Is this an example of strawperson? Why or why not?

Watching television is not good for children. Television offers nothing of value to young viewers. But parents allow their children to watch television because they are too wrapped up in their own lives to spend time with them. They use television as an electronic baby-sitter. But someday these parents will be sorry. They will be bailing their children out of jail because they committed some crime they learned on television.

Identify the generalizations the author uses in this paragraph.

Television—helpful or harmful?

Do you think watching television is good or bad for young people? Why?

CRITICAL THINKING SKILL 1

Identifying Propaganda Techniques

After reading the two viewpoints on television's effects on children, make a chart similar to the one made for Christopher and Kelly on page 10. List one example of each propaganda technique for each author's viewpoint. A chart is started for you below:

Author #1:

GENERALIZATION

Famous people agree that television is good for children.

Author #2:

STRAWPERSON

Defenders of "Sesame Street": By watching Cookie Monster behave like a slob, children see how disgusting he is. This keeps them from behaving like Cookie Monster.

Author: That is like saying that watching people rob banks on television will prevent children from becoming bank robbers.

After completing your chart, answer the following questions. Which viewpoint used the most propaganda techniques? Which viewpoint was the most convincing? Why? Which one did you personally agree with?

CHAPTER

PREFACE: Does Television Cause Children to Become Violent?

The number of violent acts depicted on television has risen in the past twenty years. Prime-time television reached an all-time high for violent programming in 1986. During that year, thirteen violent acts per hour were shown on television. In addition, 55 percent of programs shown were high in violence.

Along with the increase in violence on television, there has been an increase of violence in American cities. The United States now has the highest crime rate of all the industrialized nations.

Aletha Huston, a researcher who has studied the effects of television violence on children, says that this increase in violence can be traced, in part, to television. She, and others who agree with her, say that television makes children violent and aggressive.

Most psychologists and researchers admit that television violence affects some children. But they deny that it affects most children. Professor Wilbur Shramm says that a child's homelife is more important in determining whether a child is violent. According to Shramm, children who are raised in a loving home by kind, nonviolent parents are not affected by television violence. They do not commit the violent acts they see on television. On the other hand, children who are raised in abusive homes often mimic the violent acts they see on television.

The following viewpoints discuss the effects television violence has on children. Pay attention to the authors' use of strawperson and generalization.

Editor's Note: Much research has been done on the effects television violence has on children. According to this author, such violence is harmful to children because it teaches them to behave aggressively and because it desensitizes them to the violence they see around them. Does the author use propaganda techniques to persuade you?

Some children spend up to fifty-four hours a week watching television. During prime-time viewing, they witness five acts of violence an hour. On the weekends, the rate of violence is even higher. Twenty violent acts occur each hour on weekend television.

These incidences of television violence have an effect on children. Children model their behavior after violent characters. One group of teenagers poured gasoline over a homeless person and ignited it because they had seen it done on television.

Do all children model their behavior after violent characters? Is this a generalization?

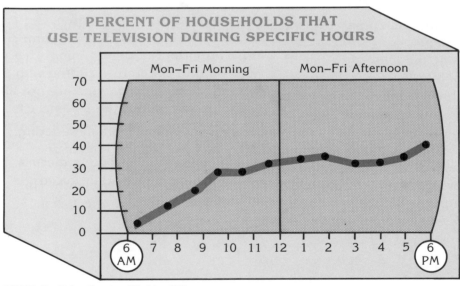

PERCENT OF HOUSEHOLDS THAT USE TELEVISION DURING SPECIFIC HOURS

SOURCE: The Nielsen Report on Television 1980

If violence was limited to adult programming, the problem may not be so serious. Parents could just supervise their children's viewing habits. They could allow their children to watch only certain television programs. But violence is not limited to shows intended for adults. Violence occurs in children's shows, including cartoons.

Wily Coyote is always trying to blow up the roadrunner. Elmer Fudd's main purpose in life is to shoot poor old Bugs Bunny and cook him for dinner. Children learn to be violent from these cartoon shows. And the fact that these shows are intended for children indicates that television producers do not use common sense when they plan their programming.

Identify the generalizations in this paragraph.

Television violence is harmful to children and to society in general because it desensitizes them to violence. That is, children who see a lot of violence on television stop thinking violence is wrong.

A study proves that children can become desensitized to violence. Researchers used machines to measure children's heart beat, perspiration, and breathing while they watched television. The children who had not watched television for two years showed rapid heart beat and breathing as well as excessive perspiration while watching a violent television show. This indicated that the violence was affecting them. On the other hand, children who had watched a lot of television prior to the test showed no change in bodily functions. This proves that the violence had little effect on them. Some experts believe that this study proves that children who watch a lot of television are no longer shocked by violence. Because of this, they become indifferent toward human suffering.

The author is using this study to prove a generalization she has stated. What is that generalization?

Barry Lynn is a researcher who has studied the effects of television programming on children. He disagrees that this evidence proves that television makes kids behave violently. He argues that these studies "may tell little about the effect that television has in the world outside the laboratory."

The author tells us what Lynn's opinion of the laboratory tests is. Does she then set up Lynn's argument to make it look ridiculous? Is this an example of strawperson? Why or why not?

I think Lynn should back up his argument with facts. If he thinks the lab experiments are inaccurate, he should do some experiments of his own. His argument, as he presents it, simply implies that television *may* not do something. It does not tell us what television does or does not do for sure.

Some people argue that television might not be harmful to most children. They say that if a child has been raised in a loving home by gentle, caring parents, chances are good that he or she will not be affected by television violence. Wilbur Shramm, a college professor, defends this argument. He says that children who have not known violence and hostility in their personal lives will probably not be influenced by television violence to commit violent acts.

Mike Luckovich for the Atlanta Constitution. Reprinted with permission.

This argument does not make much sense to me. Shramm is implying that only emotionally disturbed children are affected by television violence. But research indicates that all children learn from what they see going on in the world around them. And television brings them pictures of this world. To say that somehow "normal" children can block out lessons dealing with violence is incorrect. These children learn as much about violence from television as any other children do.

Television violence can harm children. It is time that we, as parents and teachers, demand that television networks stop broadcasting violent programs.

Read Shramm's argument carefully. Then read the author's rebuttal to the argument carefully. Does the author somehow distort Shramm's argument? If so, how?

Television violence

Violence includes physical force used to hurt a person or animal. It also includes physical force used to abuse material objects, such as breaking windows in a house just for fun. Do you ever watch television programs, including cartoons, that contain acts of violence? What are these acts of violence? How do you feel when you see violence on television?

Editor's Note: This viewpoint argues that television violence may not be harmful to children. In fact, it may help children release frustration and other strong emotions. According to this author, television violence also teaches children that violence hurts everyone, including the person committing the violent act. What types of propaganda techniques does the author use to convince you that he is right?

The question "Does television cause violence in children?" is being debated by every member of our society. Some people say that it does. Dr. Victor B. Cline, professor of psychology at the University of Utah, agrees. He said that studies have shown that "televised and filmed violence can. . .trigger. . .violent behavior."

Dr. Cline bases his belief that television causes violent behavior on laboratory experiments done in the 1970s. In these experiments, some children were shown violent television programs. Others were shown nonviolent programs. Then they were all sent into a room to play together. The children who were shown violent television programs were more violent than children who were not.

These experiments do not prove that television teaches children to behave violently. The children who were more violent in the laboratory may not be more violent in the real world. No one followed the children around to see if they behaved violently outside the laboratory. Also, the tests showed that children who saw the violent programs played more roughly with toys but not more roughly with other children.

It may be that television violence affects children. But the effect is not necessarily bad. In fact, television violence is good for children. It helps them release their feelings of anger and frustration.

The Greeks were the first to realize that people can release their own feelings by watching other people release theirs. This is called "catharsis." Greek actors performed in plays in which they acted out strong feelings such as anger and fear. To release these feelings, they often committed violent acts, including murder. Audience members indentified with the actors and pretended they were committing the violent acts. By doing this, they were able to release strong emotions such as anger. The Greeks believed that if people release these emotions by watching the actors, they would not be violent themselves.

What argument does the author use to dispute Dr. Cline's claim? Is this a valid argument or is it an example of strawperson? Why?

Which propaganda technique does the author use in this paragraph?

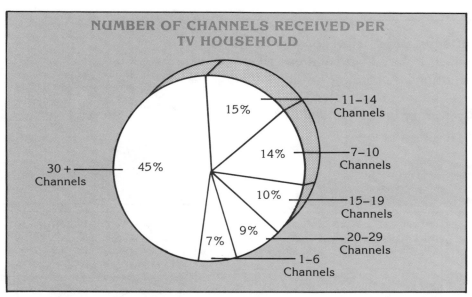

NUMBER OF CHANNELS RECEIVED PER TV HOUSEHOLD

- 11–14 Channels
- 7–10 Channels
- 15–19 Channels
- 20–29 Channels
- 1–6 Channels
- 30 + Channels

15%
14%
10%
45%
9%
7%

SOURCE: The Nielsen Report on Television 1988

Modern television programs have the same cathartic effect on today's children. Watching a character release strong emotions through violence helps children release their own strong feelings.

For example, the Incredible Hulk is actually an ordinary man who becomes a powerful green monster when his feelings are aroused. He is able to use his strength to make people do things he wants them to do. He is also able to punish people who hurt him. By identifying with the Hulk, children feel powerful. They are able to release the feelings of fear, anger, and weakness that often accompany being small and helpless.

Psychologists agree that television helps children release feelings. Jerome Lopiparo, a child psychologist, says, "Many of the frustrations they (children) feel can be very effectively worked out via the TV screen."

Watching television violence can also benefit children in another way. It teaches children that violent behavior often causes more pain to the person committing the behavior than to the victim. For example, Wily Coyote, the cartoon character, uses violence in his attempt to capture the roadrunner. He tries to flatten the roadrunner with boulders. He tries to blow him up with dynamite. But everything he tries backfires, and it is Wily who ends up being flattened and blown up.

Identify the generalization in this paragraph. What example is used to prove this generalization? Does it prove that the generalization is true in all cases?

Identify the generalization in this paragraph. What proof does the author use to prove that this generalization is always true?

What is the author hoping to prove by citing this example? Is this an example of a propaganda technique? If so, which one?

Television violence might be good for society as well as for children. It might influence them to look for peaceful ways to solve differences. By seeing the violence of war depicted on television, children might grow up to work for peace. By seeing examples of people's injustice toward one another, children may grow up to fight injustice.

People who argue that television violence teaches children violent behavior have not given the subject much thought. Neala S. Schwartzberg, a psychologist, believes television causes children to become more violent. She says television shows "are so vivid and convincing that they affect [children's] thoughts and ideas." If Schwartzberg gave the subject a little more thought, she would realize that television does not turn children into crazed killers. What television does do is help children release their feelings rather than commit a violent act.

Is this an example of strawperson? Why or why not?

Alternatives to violence

Using the Incredible Hulk as an example, the author implies that television characters use violence to get their way. What other methods could you use to convince people to do things your way?

Identifying Propaganda Techniques in Editorial Cartoons

Throughout this book, you have seen cartoons that illustrate the ideas in the viewpoints. Editorial cartoons are an effective and usually humorous way of presenting an opinion on an issue. Cartoonists sometimes use generalizations in their cartoons. That is, they imply that the idea presented by the cartoon is always the case.

Look at the cartoon below. To understand the generalization the cartoonist is making, you need to understand that the figures floating around the TV antenna are meant to represent the types of shows television offers. Look at these figures. Why does the cartoonist use the caption "air pollution" on the cartoon? What types of shows does the cartoonist believe are available on television? What generalization is he making about television programs? Can you think of any other types of shows, besides the ones represented here, that television offers?

For further practice, look at the editorial cartoons in your daily newspaper. Try to decide if the cartoonist is generalizing about a subject in the cartoon.

AIR POLLUTION

CHAPTER

PREFACE: Should Television Be
Used in the Classroom?

Many children willingly spend an average of thirty hours a week in front of a television set. Some educators believe they can use this to their advantage. Since children like to sit in front of the television, teachers can use them in classrooms to show educational programs. The children will watch the programs and will learn from them.

Other educators believe that television should not be used in the classroom as a teaching aid. They say that television makes teachers' jobs harder instead of easier. Children become used to being entertained by the fast-paced action of television programs. Then they become bored by the slow, steady pace of the classroom teacher. One teacher, comparing herself to the educational program "Sesame Street," described her frustrations: "I can't compete with television. I can't change my body into different letters, nor can I change colors. The lessons I consider exciting fall flat because I don't do these phenomenal things."

The next two viewpoints reach opposite conclusions about the use of television in the classroom. Take note of the propaganda techniques each author uses.

Editor's Note: In this viewpoint, the author argues that because children like to watch television, they will be attentive to lessons taught on television in the classroom. She says these lessons could be entertaining as well as educational. What types of propaganda techniques does the author use to support her argument?

Locate the generalizations in this paragraph.

Television can and should be used in the classroom to teach children. Watching television is entertaining. By using it in the classroom, teachers can get children to pay attention. Children are used to paying close attention to a television screen. It is easy to get them involved in an educational program on a classroom television.

Is this a strawperson argument? Why or why not?

Not everyone would agree that a classroom television is a good idea. For example, communications professor Neil Postman argues that it is not good for children to "sit transfixed in front of a television screen." "Transfixed," according to the dictionary, means "to make motionless." It seems to me that getting children to sit transfixed in front of the television screen would be helpful to an educator. It would allow the teacher to perform important duties like grading papers and preparing lessons.

Television could also be helpful in the classroom because of the quality of educational programs that might be shown. A U.S. history lesson could be filmed at a studio. Actors could dress up in colonial costumes. Historical dramas, such as the signing of the Declaration of Independence, could be enacted. Such lessons would be more meaningful to students than simply reading words and looking at pictures.

Reprinted with special permission of North American Syndicate, Inc.

Other subjects too would be more exciting if television were used to teach these subjects. Science is an example. Science teachers do not have money to buy supplies to demonstrate experiments. But these experiments could be filmed in a studio with dramatic lighting and elaborate props. Everyday, at a specified time, exciting science programs could be broadcast. Each program could teach a new science topic, such as why volcanoes erupt. Not only would these shows be educational, but they would also be entertaining. Teachers could follow up with a lesson on the same topic as the TV program showed.

Besides teaching science and other subjects, television also generates children's desire to read more books. A study done in New Jersey proves this. Forty percent of the third graders in one school chose to read books that had been made into films. Included were *Little House on the Prairie* and *Sounder*.

Television instruction can be helpful to both students and teachers. When the television becomes the instructor, the teacher is free to spend time with students who need extra help. This not only helps the students but also helps the teachers. Television can make it easier for teachers to address the needs of all their students.

Television will probably never replace teachers in the classroom. But it can help the teachers do their jobs more efficiently. Most teachers do not have time to entertain their students. They cannot change costumes to present history lessons. They do not have time to construct exciting science demonstrations every day. And they cannot act out entire plays so that children will be inspired to read books. Television can do all this because its purpose is to entertain as well as instruct.

The idea that education could be entertaining bothers some people. Professor Neil Postman is one such person. He said, "No one has ever said or implied that significant learning is . . . achieved when education is entertainment." Postman and others who argue against entertainment in education seem convinced that learning must be boring. I think Postman is wrong. I think learning can be fun and that television can help make it fun.

Does the author use a propaganda technique in this paragraph? If so, which one?

What does the author hope to prove by citing this statistic? Is this a propaganda technique? If so, which one?

Does the author use a propaganda technique here? If so, which one?

Television and reading

Have you ever watched a television program and read the book with the same title, such as *Little House on the Prairie*? Did watching the program help you understand the story better than just reading the book? How?

Editor's Note: In this viewpoint, the author argues that if television were used as a teacher, children would be harmed both emotionally and academically. Be aware of the propaganda techniques the author uses to support his argument.

Identify the generalization in this paragraph. How does the author try to prove that this generalization is always true?

Is this a generalization? Why or why not?

American children spend over four hours a day watching television. A study done in New York City proves this. According to this study, New York children from two to five years old watch thirty hours of television each week. Six- to eleven-year-olds in New York spend over twenty-five hours a day watching television. If television becomes a classroom instructor, some children will be spending over half of their waking hours glued to a television set.

Watching this much television can be bad for children for many reasons. One reason is that watching television takes time away from other activities that are important in childhood development. For example, children need to spend time playing with other children to develop their social skills.

Using television as a teacher can be bad for children for emotional as well as physical reasons. In order to learn, students must have a good relationship with their teacher. They must feel that the teacher cares about them. If the teacher is off in a corner grading papers while the students are watching television, this close relationship cannot develop.

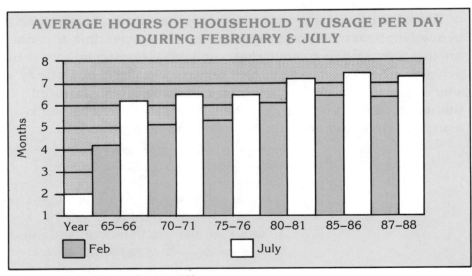

SOURCE: The Nielsen Report on Television 1988

Finally, television instruction is bad for children because it is ineffective. Children do not learn from television. One study showed that children remember less than 2 percent of the facts they learned from one television program.

Some people argue that television is a good classroom instructor because it helps students learn to read. Patricia Greenfield, a psychology professor, says "Television and film can...be used to enhance the comprehension and enjoyment of literature."

I disagree with Greenfield. When children spend all their time in front of the television, they do not learn to read. They never have a chance to enhance their reading skills because they have not learned them in the first place.

Another argument people use to defend television in the classroom is that television makes education entertaining. This may be true, but students learn something more than the subject being taught. They learn to expect to be entertained all the time. Then when students get tired of watching television, they seek dangerous entertainment. This includes taking drugs.

Great educators throughout history have said many things about education. They have said it was necessary in order to understand life. They have said it should be available to all people. They have said it should continue throughout a person's life. But they have never said it had to be entertaining.

I have heard teachers defend the use of television in the classroom. They say that if students spend an hour or two a day watching an educational program, teachers could spend time with students who are slower learners and need extra help.

But all students need individual attention. Faster learners need as much special attention as slower learners. I agree that it is not fair to expect slow learners to keep up with the lessons the rest of the class is working on. But I also think it is unfair that fast learners have to waste time on lessons that they have already learned. If teachers had to cater to each student's individual needs, they would spend all day on individual lessons.

Television does not help children learn. Nor does it help them to love education. It only teaches them to love television.

Does the author use a propaganda technique in this paragraph? If so, which one?

Is this an example of the strawperson technique? Why or why not?

Which propaganda technique does the author use in this paragraph? How do you know?

Is this a propaganda technique? If so, which one?

Does television make learning interesting?

Think of a subject you are learning in school that might be more interesting if it were taught on television. How could television make this subject more interesting?

This activity will allow you to practice identifying propaganda techniques. The statements below focus on the subject matter of this book. They may be examples of generalizations or strawperson. In part I, mark a "G" next to any statement you believe is a generalization. In part II, mark a "S" next to the rebuttals to the arguments that you believe are examples of strawperson.

Part I: *Answer*

EXAMPLE: All children who watch television lack social   G
skills.

1. People spend too much time watching television.   ———

2. Watching television makes children violent.   ———

3. Isaac Asimov believes that television teaches   ———
   children many useful lessons.

Part II

Original Argument: Television programs today contain too much violence. Children learn from this violence. They learn to hit their brothers and sisters and to break their toys when they get angry. Television, above all other causes, is most to blame for violence in children.

Rebuttal: It is true that some programs contain violence. And perhaps children do learn violent behavior from these programs. But television is not the main cause of violence in children. Society itself teaches children violence. A person need only pick up a newspaper to see that we live in a violent society. Children learn more about violence from the people they share this planet with than they do from television.

Original Argument: I do not think we should spend money putting television sets in every classroom. Television is not going to make education more interesting. I never liked science in school, and no television program was going to make science interesting to me.

Rebuttal: This argument really makes me angry. Some people have no problems with spending money on defense. But when it comes to education, they do not want to spend any money at all.